THE ART OF
Reading
Images

Pari

notionpress.com
INDIA · SINGAPORE · MALAYSIA

ISBN 979-8-89588-924-4

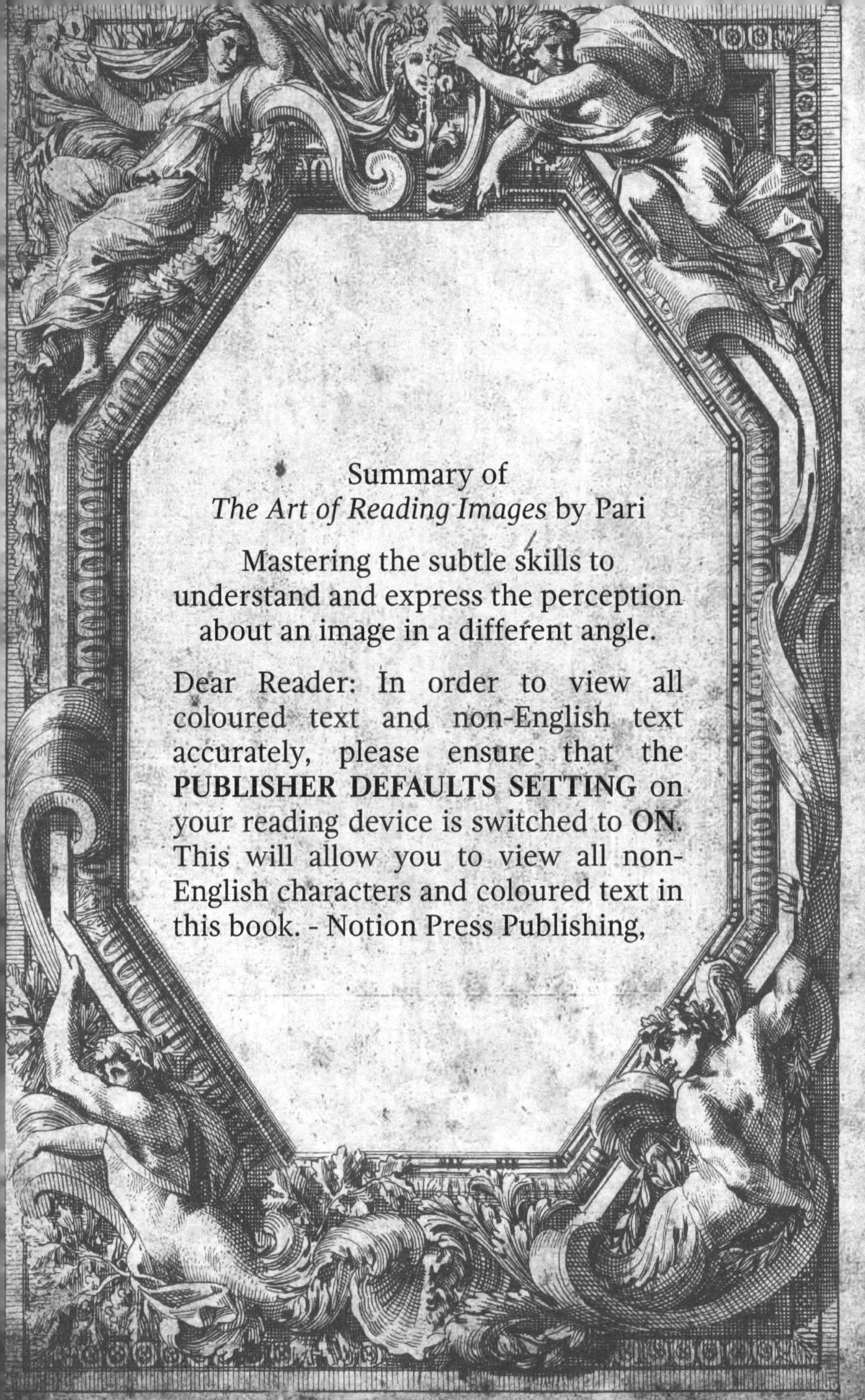

Summary of
The Art of Reading Images by Pari

Mastering the subtle skills to understand and express the perception about an image in a different angle.

Dear Reader: In order to view all coloured text and non-English text accurately, please ensure that the **PUBLISHER DEFAULTS SETTING** on your reading device is switched to **ON**. This will allow you to view all non-English characters and coloured text in this book. - Notion Press Publishing,

Contents

Acknowledgments...6
Preface...7

The Eye of the Soul..14
Glass Window...20
Broken Mirror..28
Love Yourself..34
The Calmest Sea..42
Words Fail to Speak..48
Messenger of God..58

Epilogue...65
References...70

Acknowledgments

I am incredibly grateful to all of the people and things that have made writing *The Art of Reading Images* possible. It has been a truly enlightening and life-changing experience for me.

First and foremost, I would like to express my sincere gratitude to Krishnavanie Shunmugam, my mentor and leader, whose support and knowledge have served as a continual source of inspiration. Unceasing mentorship has influenced my comprehension of visual literacy and paved the way for this work.

My family and friends, I am very grateful for your unwavering belief in my endeavour and your support. This book wouldn't exist without your tolerance during the endless hours I spent researching and writing, as well as your enlightening criticism.

A special thank you to the hardworking staff at Notion Press Publishing, whose enthusiasm and expertise saw this book through to completion. We sincerely appreciate your rigorous attention to detail and dedication to quality.

Finally, I would like to express my gratitude to you, the audience and reader, for joining me on this journey. What makes this project valuable is your willingness to interact with and learn about the skill of image reading. It is my desire that this book will broaden your understanding of visual art and encourage you to view the world with an open mind and fresh eyes.

With gratitude,
[Pari]

Preface

Being able to genuinely "read" an image has become a rare and valuable skill in today's society where visual stimuli assault us from all sides. There are a plethora of images, graphics, and designs in our environment, all competing for our attention and interpretation. How often, though, do we stop to think about the complexity and subtlety that each image contains? How many of you often interact with visual art in a way that goes beyond just viewing?

The Art of Reading Images explores how looking at images through a lens free of preconceptions can have a transforming effect. All readers are invited by this book to adopt a technique that goes beyond traditional analysis and asks you to reveal the hidden layers of meaning. Reading pictures objectively is also more than just a passive observation exercise; it's a dynamic art form that develops creativity, sharpens problem-solving skills, and cultivates a more profound awareness of the world. We discover hidden truths and develop an appreciation for different viewpoints when we approach images with curiosity and an open mind.

You are going to go on a journey that defies conventional interpretation boundaries when you turn the pages of this book. You'll learn how to interact with images in a way that stimulates new perspectives and creative thought. Every page offers a different investigation into how we might develop a more creative and perceptive approach to the pictures that are all around us.

Regardless of your background – artist, student, professional, or just an inquisitive observer – this book provides strategies and resources to improve your visual literacy. It challenges you to go beyond the apparent, to inquire, and to delve deeper. Learning to read images can help you see how every visual experience may be used as a blank canvas for introspection and artistic expression.

Let's embrace the skill of viewing images with awe and possibility, and let's see the limitless possibilities that each frame has.

Greetings from a different angle. This is *The Art of Reading Images*. Welcome.

How It Works::

"*The Art of Reading Images*" offers a compelling exploration of the dynamic relationship between visual and textual interpretation. This method invites readers to engage with visual content first, before delving into written passages, providing a unique framework for understanding how images shape perception and meaning. Each practice within this book presents an opportunity to uncover new ways of seeing, encouraging a deeper understanding that may differ from my own perspective yet still hold profound value.

I am confident that this book will inspire you to carefully examine each image, allowing you to uncover its hidden significance. In times of challenge, your unique perspective can illuminate new possibilities for others, offering fresh insights that may positively impact their lives. As a writer and communicator, you may find this approach invaluable, not only in capturing your readers' attention but also in helping them engage more deeply with the ideas and viewpoints you present.

Never underestimate the power of your words. What you share has the potential to resonate far beyond what you may realise, influencing hearts and minds in ways that can inspire change. The wisdom and knowledge granted to us by God—intended to nurture peace and harmony in the world—should echo louder than ever before. By guiding your readers to view and interpret images in a way that fosters understanding, you can help lead them toward a life marked by greater harmony, insight, and purpose.

Initial Engagement with Visual Content:

1.Begin by closely examining the images presented in the book. Pay careful attention to their various elements—such as colors, shapes, figures, and any prominent details—to form your own interpretation.

2.Reflect on your initial impressions and emotions upon viewing the images. Consider what feelings or thoughts emerge, as these insights can serve as a foundation for your writing. This technique can also act as an engaging hook to interact with your audience.

Forming Perceptions:

1. Write down your personal perception of the images. This might include your interpretations of what the images represent, any narratives they suggest, and how they relate to your own experiences or knowledge.

2. For each image and text, consider the context of the image. Are there historical, cultural, or social aspects that might influence your perception? Why do some images seem "good" while others may not?

Reading the Passages:

After forming your initial impressions, carefully read the passages that are related. These texts frequently offer more background or offer different perspectives on the same photographs. It could include both your interpretation and the same one. Even if your understanding differs from mine, you can still find a fresh path to go when conducting new study.

Examine your interpretations against what the passages say. Make a note of any confirmations or differences. In what ways does the text change or impact how you interpret the images?

The term "read" is often used interchangeably with "interpret," but it carries the added benefit of emphasising the visual aspect of comprehension through both the eyes and the mind. "Reading" can take on various meanings: it may simply refer to "deciphering" or "decoding," but it can also underscore the interpretive effort, suggesting terms such as "making intelligible," "revealing the internal logic of," or "forming a perspective." When we speak of "reading images," we are referring to the process of analysing both form and content, examining how they interact, while also considering the context in which an image was created and perceived (Sears & Thomas, 2002, p. 1).

According to Kress and Van Leeuwen (2010), multimodal social semiotics not only focuses on the means of making meaning but also on the very nature of those means. Whether through language, images, gestures, or sounds, multimodal semiotics seeks to understand how these modes contribute to meaning-making.

The process of image interpretation is an ordered sequence that includes detection, recognition, identification, classification, and analysis (Danny, p. 7). The human brain draws upon stored experiences that allow us to recognise objects, based on prior learning and knowledge. The more we observe images and reflect inwardly, the deeper we can discover insights about ourselves and our lives, as images can serve as mirrors to our souls (Gerd Ziegler, 1986, p. 8).

A social semiotic approach centers on the repertoire of signals available for communication and how they are used in context to convey broader concepts, attitudes, and emotions. It also explores the reasons behind the choices made in creating these signals. Elements such as colour, shape, and their interaction within a visual design are of particular interest to this approach. However, very few linguists adhere to the extreme view that language dictates our worldview; instead, they argue that language influences, but does not entirely determine, the way we perceive the world. This view aligns with the Sapir-Whorf hypothesis, which suggests that people involved in communication agree to use the same words to convey the same meanings, with these words serving as arbitrary symbols that do not inherently refer to external reality.

Multimodal social semiotics further examines how meaning is constructed through various modes—whether language, images, gestures, or sounds (Kress, 2010, p. 45). The goal of Multimodal Critical Discourse Analysis (MCDA) is to demonstrate how visual elements such as pictures, photos, diagrams, and graphics contribute to meaning-making. These visual and linguistic techniques, while seemingly neutral or ordinary, may carry ideological underpinnings designed to influence how people and events are represented for particular purposes (Machin & Mayr, 2012, p. 63).

Images themselves can be both denotative (literal) or connotative (symbolic), depending on the context in which they are used (Machin & Mayr, 2012, p. 56). In this analysis, I will explore images that illustrate pragmatic and semiotic concepts, focusing on various elements of image interpretation. Charles Forceville stresses the importance of training individuals to interpret images, noting that their "grammar" is not universal and primarily accounts for images in Western societies. Forceville also criticizes Kress and Leeuwen for insufficiently discussing how their defined visual markers relate to one another and can be practically applied in the analysis of specific images.

A functional approach to image analysis, as outlined by Kress and Van Leeuwen (1990 & 1996), observes images through 3 distinct "metafunctions." These include the 'what' (how reality is represented in the images) and the 'who' (how the images are arranged). Visuals, like any form of representation, are never neutral reflections of reality. Rather than simply mirroring the world, they provide interpretations of it (Midalia, 1999, p. 131). Consequently, viewers are prompted to ask: "How can we justify and ground the meaning(s) of the picture?"

Visuals, therefore, are never true representations of reality or truth; they always reflect a particular perspective. This perspective is shaped by factors such as cultural background and individual experiences. For

example, consider the image of a fruit. Different people might interpret it differently. Would everyone choose the same fruit? Similarly, when considering the image of a dog, while most might view it as a companion or pet, others might perceive it as a threat or even as food, depending on their cultural or personal experiences. This illustrates how the interpretation of images varies widely based on worldview and cultural background.

The key takeaway from this is that there are multiple ways to create and convey images (Jonathan S. Marlon & Jerome W. Crowser, 2013, p. 32). In visual research, there is no single "right way" to analyse images. Context is crucial, and the same visual research can look vastly different depending on the issue, location, and approach, as demonstrated by the variety of case studies.

"The Images of the Environment" suggest that every image contains more than meets the eye—more than can be heard by the ear (Kevin Lynch,1990, p. 6). Each image holds a setting or a viewpoint waiting to be explored. Lynch explains that images are soaked in memories and meanings, produced by both immediate sensation and the memory of past experiences. These images are used to interpret information and guide action (Lynch, 1990, p. 8).

It is also important to acknowledge that the lighting conditions under which we view historical art, images, and colours have changed significantly compared to the lighting conditions of ancient and medieval societies. Modern societies experience these images in a very different way (Gardes Collees, 2008, p. 8). Kress and Van Leeuwen argue that visuals offer a rich and distinctive means of communication. They encourage scholars of visual communication to "develop theory related to representation and rhetoric based on what is seen rather than what is spoken."

The Art of
READing
Images

The Eye of the Soul

In The Republic, Socrates posits that education involves directing the soul's attention toward worthwhile ideas. Intellectuals often interpret Plato's allegory of the cave as a metaphor for the separation from the shadows of everyday existence. This allegory the individual's attachment—or lack thereof—to the pleasures and desires driven by the irascible and appetitive aspects of the psyche. It highlights the distinction between those who remain fixated on the shadows and those who look upwards toward the truth, aligning their souls with their intellects.

Plato's cave allegory describes four stages of imprisonment: (1) the life of prisoners chained at the bottom of the cave; (2) the liberation of one prisoner who ascends towards the light; (3) the realisation of realities previously hidden, including the Form of the Good; and (4) the return to the cave to engage in political life. In the cave, individuals live in isolation, unable to move freely. Their understanding of reality is limited to a distorted version, 3 degrees removed from true reality, and they remain unaware of the truths around them, obscured by the shadows cast by puppeteers.

Plato illustrates the difficulty of the liberation process. Even after a prisoner is freed, mental suffering does not cease immediately. The only way for the prisoner to escape is to be "dragged into the light of day," a process that can be painful. This moment of liberation involves 2 distinct actions: escaping and choosing to turn toward the light. The pain associated with this extraordinary upheaval sharply contrasts with the lesser quality of experiences within the cave. Ultimately, the freed prisoner may choose to remain in the cave to avoid the discomfort of confronting a new reality.

The image of a flower and its leaves can symbolise the spirit of nature. However, upon closer inspection, the absence of eyes in these representations highlights the disconnect of the viewer from deeper understanding. Audiences rarely question why the leaves lack eyes, and thus the soul's attention is not directed toward meaningful contemplation. True wisdom involves more than sharp vision; it requires the ability to recognise what is essential and to respond with moral integrity. This necessitates harmony within the soul, where reason governs emotions and desires, aligning the entire soul toward virtuous deeds.

Plato argues that even those in the cave who can clearly see the shadows (the "eyes") are not truly wise. While their understanding of the shadows may be sharp, it does not equate to true knowledge. The "eye of providence" serves as a metaphor for divine oversight, suggesting that the images we perceive can have multiple interpretations and meanings. In the context of the "eye of the soul," semiotic phenomenology seeks to describe, thematise, and interpret the structures of communication that emerge within our being. The perception of phenomena reveals their meanings, while expression imbues them with significance. This approach is particularly relevant when exploring the nature of images. The foundational question we must ask is: "What does it mean to see an image?" This leads to further inquiries: What does it mean to see? How does seeing acquire meaning? Who is the seeing subject, and what is being observed?

Semiotic phenomenology begins with the immediate act of viewing, performed by an embodied subject within a shared world. This foundational act of perception enables the intelligibility and communication of images, grounding secondary semiotic frameworks (Sobchack, 1992, p. 10). The act of "seeing-in-the-world" underpins the existential act of seeing the world with one's own eyes (Sobchack, 1992, p. 51). To see with one's eyes is accessible to animals and infants, but to see with one's own eyes—as an "I"—implies reflexivity and situational awareness. Neither animals nor infants consciously situate themselves in the world; they perceive it as visible, but do not recognise their own position within it as the "here, where I am."

Engaging in an act of seeing that reflects on seeing requires knowledge of what it means to be both a seeing subject and a visible object.

Sobchack notes that while a baby experiences seeing, it does not yet perceive "things" as we do. Its eyes are not attuned to recognising acts of seeing. This understanding arises from the lived body, allowing the subject to represent itself to consciousness as an "I." Over time, the baby learns to recognise images not through conscious will or trained skill, but through its innate capacity for vision.

The meaning, value, and ethical significance of what we see cannot be detached from the act of seeing as a mode of knowledge or from the existential connection with the perceiving being. To direct intellectual abilities toward the good rather than the evil, education must encompass both soul transformation and cognitive development. Redirecting the soul toward the good is essential to metastrofi (transformation) in education. Without a moral compass, wisdom can become dangerous. The Allegory of the Cave illustrates that true wisdom requires deeper understanding and moral alignment; mere academic proficiency is insufficient.

The Art of
READING
Images

Glass Window

New perspectives on visual representations of objects and environments can help communicate larger ideas (Machin & Mayr, 2012, p. 102). For over a millennium, English churches and cathedrals have used painted and stained glass windows to tell historical tales and depict significant events. These vibrant windows—whether massive and imposing or small and delicate—offer more than religious symbolism; they also serve as striking records of the people whose beliefs and passions shaped England throughout the ages. The art of stained glass, often referred to as painting with light, has long inspired viewers.

As early as AD 669–672, window glass was introduced at York Minster to prevent birds and rain from entering. According to a twelfth-century manuscript, the glass was processed and cut into small shapes, or "quarries," such as squares, rectangles, triangles, diamonds, and curves. These pieces were then assembled into intricate patterns, often held together by lead strips (Rosewell, 1860, p. 8).

While clear (white) glass was produced in the Wealden forests of Surrey and Kent from the thirteenth to the seventeenth centuries, evidence of glass production in England during the Anglo-Saxon period is scarce. Despite this, the practice of interpreting and analyzing window glass remains a fascinating exercise. When interpreting glass windows, one might describe their size, shape, design, and color, yet a deeper analysis reveals that the meanings these windows convey are often more subtle, requiring careful interpretation (Machin & Mayr, 2012, p. 36).

When we explore the way objects and settings in images carry meanings, it's essential to recognise that these meanings are often not immediately apparent. For instance, a window might be viewed as simply a piece of glass in a frame, but deeper analysis could uncover underlying cultural or historical significance. These interpretations might be implicit—suggesting ideas or beliefs without explicitly stating them. Implicit meanings are part of a mental model but are not directly asserted in the text. (Van Dijk, 2001, p. 104)

The way we interpret visual images often depends on shared cultural assumptions. For example, a "glass window" involves assumptions about what "glass" and "window" are. We take these assumptions for granted, but examining them more closely can reveal unexpected interpretations. The act of naming or classifying objects, such as a "glass window," involves choices that are shaped by cultural norms and historical contexts.

When considering the phrase "glass window," it's worth asking why we choose to name it in this way. What combination of terms—such as "glass window" or "window glass"—best represents the object? This decision reflects not only linguistic choices but also the cultural and historical associations tied to glass and windows.

Consider the two phrases:

"Take a look at the glass window!"
"Observe the glass and window!"

In which of these would you focus on one word to describe the image? "Window glass" may evoke two distinct ideas: the glass itself and the frame that holds it. If you were asked to explain the difference between these 2 objects to someone blindfolded, you would likely need to focus on their essential properties: one is transparent, and the other is structural. Through rhetoric and visual representation, these different elements can be framed in various ways to highlight certain characteristics or meanings.

"Glass and Brick Stone. Both met in the same place without hesitation"

Metaphors play a powerful role in shaping our understanding of concepts, often by transferring knowledge from one realm to another (Lakoff, 1993; Lakoff & Núñez, 1997). A metaphor can conceal or reveal meanings, shaping our perceptions and ideologies. For example, the phrase "Glass and brick stone. Both met in the same place without hesitation" carries a metaphorical implication. On one level, it might represent the collision of 2 incompatible elements, suggesting a lack of safety. On another level, it might reflect the harmony that can arise when seemingly opposite forces come together.

The metaphor "Glass and brick stone. Both met in the same place without hesitation" could be seen as a reflection of two seemingly incompatible forces that, despite their differences, find common ground. In this sense, it suggests that there are moments in life when individuals or situations may not align perfectly, but they can still coexist and create something meaningful. The image captures the idea that, while there may be friction or discomfort, some relationships or experiences are imperfectly perfect.

"People Who Live in Glass Houses Shouldn't Throw Stones"

The famous idiom "People who live in glass houses shouldn't throw stones" implies that one should not criticize others for faults that one might also have. The phrase cleverly uses the metaphor of glass and stone to suggest the vulnerability of those who live in a fragile situation and the potential harm they could cause by throwing stones—both literally and figuratively. The combination of glass and stone in this context evokes the fragility of the glass and the potential danger of the stone, highlighting the consequences of one's actions.

The idiom reflects how we understand human behavior and the consequences of actions. Just as glass is fragile and stones can shatter it, the idiom suggests that any negative action taken by a person can come back to harm them. In a world of increasing technological complexity, where glass is often used in modern architecture, this metaphor remains relevant, emphasizing the vulnerability and consequences of our actions.

The Relationship with Japanese Proverbs

There is an interesting connection between the metaphor of glass and stone and 2 Japanese proverbs:

"絵に描いた餅は食えぬ" (E ni kaita mochi wa kuenu) – "You can't eat the rice cake in a picture"

This proverb suggests that while something might look appealing in an image, it cannot provide real satisfaction. It's a reminder not to confuse art with life. Similarly, images of glass windows or other representations can appear beautiful but may not provide the deeper truth or fulfillment that reality offers. Plato's view in the Sophist aligns with this, where he states that art, though beautiful, often sacrifices truth for beauty (Boeri et al., 2018, p. 28).

"無用の用" (Muyōnoyō) – "A use for the useless"

This proverb means that even something seemingly useless can have value. This is similar to the metaphor of the glass and stone, where the 2 elements might seem incompatible at first glance but can coexist and even have a deeper purpose when combined. It reflects the idea that things or concepts often contain hidden value that may not be immediately apparent, just as the metaphorical meaning of "glass and brick stone" suggests an unexpected harmony.

In both proverbs, there is an underlying message that things are not always as they seem. The value of an object, an image, or an action lies in how it is perceived and interpreted, much like how the meanings behind a "glass window" or a metaphor like "glass and brick stone" require deeper reflection.

The Art of
READING
Images

Broken Mirror

A damaged mirror is attempting to use its fragmented pieces to tell a positive story!

"I used to reflect a flawless image of a person. Now, my shattered bits have multiplied into thousands of images! Does that mean I misread what I saw? Or are they perceiving separate reflections from the mirror? I remain the same mirror I always was! What has been hurled at me is what I project. How you interpret it is entirely up to you! Mirrors reflect the world around them without passing judgment" (Gerd Ziegler, 1986, p. 8). *I'm grateful that, despite everything, I can still capture your essence. I am still valuable! Instead of blaming my pain on the stone, I choose not to dwell on how weak I am in comparison."*

It is essential to recognise that each chemical has a unique purpose and meaning in this context. If we strive to establish our identity as someone else, we may not be living fully. The essence of existence lies in making a difference in the world by being authentic and true to who you were meant to be. To ensure it remains secure, the mirror is always positioned higher than usual. However, unlike the mirror, the stone was never taken seriously and was often discarded.

Kintsugi: Embracing Brokenness

Kintsugi (金継ぎ): This concept echoes Kintsugi, which teaches us to embrace our broken parts. It is a Japanese art form that gives damaged items new life. The term Kintsugi means "golden joinery" (金 = kin for gold; 継ぎ = tsugi for joinery). This technique uses valuable materials like liquid gold, liquid silver, or lacquer coated with powdered gold to highlight the cracks, fusing the fragments of broken objects together.

A broken mirror does not mean it is no longer functional; its fractures can become beautiful. The foundation of Kintsugi is the belief that imperfections can be both beautiful and strong. By emphasising our flaws and brokenness, we can create something resilient, unique, and stunning. This art form serves as a physical metaphor for healing and transformation.

The Power of Positive Thinking

Bill Harris, a teacher and founder of the Centerpointe Research Institute, described how a student named Robert transformed his life by shifting his negative thoughts. Instead of focusing on what he didn't want or feared, he began to concentrate on what he desired. Ultimately, Robert's life changed because he adopted a positive mindset. He projected a different frequency into the universe, which responded to his new instructions, regardless of how challenging his circumstances seemed. Robert's optimistic outlook on life became his new frequency, painting his existence vibrantly to match this new perspective. The secret of the book teaches us that the life we wish to live is in our hands.

No matter where you are or how dire your situation may seem, promise yourself that it will not remain the same. When storms arise, they will dissipate, just like clouds in the sky. You may feel as though your existence is heavy and gloomy, like the largest storm cloud. However, after the storm passes, clarity will return, and light and brightness will illuminate everything. To create change in your life, you must begin crafting your thoughts intentionally and accurately. The universe awaits your instructions to elevate you.

The Power of Belief

The only thing we often hesitate to practice is BELIEVING. It's strange that we resist accepting this truth: your life's circumstances are all subject to change! (Byrne, R., 2018, p. 19). The predominant thoughts you hold are reflected in your life. You possess the capacity to consciously think and create everything in your reality. The ability to discern artistic merit hidden behind a broken mirror and breathe new life into its images is known as creative thinking. It serves as a reminder that while difficult experiences do occur in our lives, we have the power to create something beautiful.

The Art of
READING
Images

Love Yourself

love is putting someone else's
needs before yours

Cartoons, in particular, have the unique ability to stylise and exaggerate both individual and stereotypical group traits. Machin and Thornborrow (2003) argue that these representations should be interpreted similarly to children's fairy tales. Although set in fantastical contexts, cartoons convey practical lessons about evaluating identities, concepts, morals, and behaviors that can have broader societal implications. There are 2 important distinctions between what is communicated through words versus through visual elements (Machin and Mayr, 2012, p. 62). At the same time, texts promoting social roles not only influence identities and behaviors but also shape emotions (Van Leeuwen,2008,p. 56)

The phrase, "Love is putting someone else's needs before yours," captures an emotional essence and provides valuable lessons about love, but it falls short of encapsulating the true goal of mutual affection. While prioritising the needs of others is admirable, it is equally important to emphasize the necessity of self-love. Love, at its core, should not be framed negatively, especially when shaping the mindset of young children. They must learn to value themselves in order to better meet the needs of others.

Do You Love Me?

A lover asked his beloved,
Do you love yourself more than you love me?
The Beloved replied,
I have died to myself, and I live for you.
I've disappeared from myself and my attributes;
I am present only for you.
I have forgotten all my learning,
But from knowing you,
I have become a scholar.
I have lost all my strength,
But from your power,

I am able.
If I love myself,
I love you;
If I love you,
I love myself.

— Rumi: Do You Love Me? (p. 35)

This poem, in its depiction of love, urges us to rethink our approach. Love, as expressed here, transcends the self and merges two souls.

"Love is a single soul inhabiting in two bodies." -Aristotle

The poems of Rumi reflect the deepest yearnings of the human heart as it searches for the divine. The emotions captured in the Farsi language radiate with a new life when translated, preserving the essence of the original. Rumi's words, both loud and clear, are well-paced and rhymed, yet rich with meaning. His poetry offers us a window into the magnificent universe of love, a universe that continues to astound, perplex, and enlighten us even after a millennium.

A Candle's Light

There is a touching illustration that symbolises love: when a candle burns down to the end of its wick, the flame may go out. Yet, the warmth and light the candle emitted continue to exist in our hearts. Similarly, even though our bodies will eventually dissolve, the love we cultivate on earth will endure long after our time has passed. The loved ones we have lost, though no longer with us, are like stars in the sky— shining brightly because their light continues to illuminate our lives (Alwa, 2020, p. 289). As Rumi expressed in his poetry, "Goodbyes are only means for those who love with their eyes." For those who love with all their heart and soul, separation does not exist. Disappearance has nothing to do with death or dusk; as the moon may disappear, it is never lost forever (Helwa, 2020, p. 289).

The Importance of Self-Love

To help others understand that their existence has purpose and meaning in this world, we must nourish and appreciate them. Could anyone truly accept that suicide is a valid decision for someone in this world? It is surprising to realize that we can only fully embrace and love ourselves when we stop trying to escape from our inner selves (Ziegler, 1986, p. 8).

Kevin Lynch suggests that an image is a by-product of past experience and is used to guide behavior and interpret information (Kevin Lynch, 1990, p. 8). Rather than dwelling on past errors, we reinterpret those experiences in a more structured manner. Similarly, visual representations help us to understand the world around us, guiding our perceptions and actions.

Visual Modality and Interpretation

According to Kress and Van Leeuwen, modality indicators in texts and images are essential for determining the credibility and accuracy of the information we receive. They argue that modality should be viewed as "interpersonal" rather than "ideational." This means that modality judgments in visual communication are influenced by what a social group believes to be true, real, or sacred. In this context, colors serve as key indicators of naturalistic modality, especially when considering the three scales of color modulation. Other significant indicators of visual modality include contextualization, representation, depth, lighting, and brightness. Visual producers can manipulate these modality options to convey specific meanings.

The terms "ater" and "niger" carry negative connotations—associated with being dirty, dismal, depressing, evil, dishonest, destructive, and lethal. In the past, air itself was sometimes viewed with such negativity

(Collees, 2008, p. 19). As a result, the image in question is often presented in black and white to evoke unpleasant and melancholy memories from the past. The background of the image reflects the indirect meaning of the statement, "Love is putting someone else's needs before yours." While this sentiment may seem lovely on the surface, the choice to depict the photograph in a nighttime setting introduces a somber tone, evoking nostalgia for earlier, perhaps more challenging times. Research indicates that the universe, in its earliest stages, was colourless or consisted only of grey, black, and white (Collees, 2008, p. 8).

The Art of
READING
Images

The Calmest Sea

Environmental images result from a dynamic, two-way process between the observer and their surroundings. The environment highlights differences and relationships, while the observer, with remarkable flexibility and in consideration of their own goals, selects, arranges, and contextualises what they observe. The resulting images both restrict and accentuate the perceived reality, and the image itself continuously interacts with the filtered perceptual information. Consequently, different viewers may have vastly divergent perceptions of the same reality.

For example, a worktable that appears disorganized to some may be easily navigated by an individual who can locate objects with ease. Conversely, an object seen for the first time may be immediately recognised and connected to the observer's past experiences, free from preconceptions (Kevin Lynch, 1990, p. 9). The image of the surrounding sea, viewed from various perspectives, illustrates this concept. As you descend deeper into the ocean, the water grows calmer, symbolizing both how far you have come and how far you still have to go. With determination, fight your battles and keep your heart pure. The concept of gaman refers to the strength of character shown by individuals who endure seemingly insurmountable challenges with dignity and patience (G. Mangali, A. David, 2018). Gaman served as an inspiration during World War II and the 2011 Tohoku earthquake and tsunami, when many demonstrated fortitude in the face of hardship and adversity.

When you look back, you will see the clearest view of your past. You may never fully realize how many people have been inspired by your strength. Keep it a secret that you have the ability to transform raindrops into an iron prison. Conceal the process by which clouds turn into beds. Keep the stars on your open rooftop a secret as well. Never claim that your beliefs are superior to everything on Earth. The pain has subsided, and you no longer feel discomfort. Instead, a heavy sense of happiness and ecstasy fills the atmosphere. You have cast your burdens into the depths of the ocean. Give yourself a break; you have been carrying this weight for years, and it is truly heavy. Your close circle may have unknowingly added to it. Set it aside and focus on what needs to be done in the present moment.

Everyone should have the opportunity to express themselves. By connecting with others, they should bring value to their surroundings. It has been a while now. You stop, look back, and realize that everything you have done is genuine. Though it may have been shattered and thrown into the deep ocean, in its depths it now resembles coral. Corals found in deep waters do not require sunlight to survive. The tears of the sea mother have purified your head and heart. She forgives you and embraces you for who you are, wrapping you in her warmth. Her healing energy permeates every part of your body. These thoughts cross your mind whenever you visit the beach or the ocean. It is there that you can reconstruct your feelings and renew your inner self.

Except for mermaids, no one can survive beneath the ocean's surface without the proper life-support equipment. "Imagination is everything," as Albert Einstein once said. Imagination offers a glimpse into life at its most beautiful. Through it, we come to understand the existence of sea coral, a plant that thrives under the deep sea. Sunlight is essential for photosynthesis, yet the deep ocean is devoid of light. Naturally, the inquisitive mind wonders how sea coral manages to perform photosynthesis at such depths. At this point, curiosity leads you to learn more about other living organisms, prompting you to investigate how coral survives in these extreme conditions.

Without external assistance, imagination guides our thinking from one place to another. In this sense, it enhances our ability to think and write creatively. It allows us to choose, arrange, and imbue the deep sea with various meanings and memories as we imagine adapting to life beneath the waves—all in the context of our personal goals. This concept of experiential meaning potential refers to the idea that signifiers derive meaning based on how we utilise them and the actions involved in their creation. It emphasizes our ability to translate experiences into knowledge, thereby symbolically broadening our understanding. This process allows us to recognise the comparable extensions made by others, helping to create shared meanings. The signs we articulate are easily perceived and interpreted by others, providing a foundation for future articulations. Over time, this process of interpretation and re-articulation transforms original meanings, making them clearer and more meaningful.

The Art of
READING
Images

Words Fail to Speak

If a part of the body hurts,
All parts contract with pain.

If you are not concerned
With another's suffering,
We shall not call you human.

(Rumi: Bridge to the Soul, What It Is to Be Human, p. 27)

The value of suffering lies in its capacity to teach us acceptance of things as they are. As the saying goes, we do not perceive things as they are, but as we are. Pain has the remarkable ability to transform a person—turning an outgoing individual into someone silent and introspective, or vice versa. This image does not aim to document the actions of a specific woman at a particular time or place; instead, it conveys a broader symbolic meaning. The creator intentionally manipulates textures and colors to different degrees, knowing that these aesthetic choices will guide the viewer's interpretation of the image as symbolic, rather than realistic.

Edgar Wind emphasizes the critical role of knowledge in understanding and appreciating the aesthetic value of images: "The eye focuses differently when it is intellectually guided." However, his statement "Our eye sees as our mind reads" captures this idea more effectively. E.H. Gombrich's contemporaries echoed similar thoughts, noting that the brain's ability to recognise a line-and-mass arrangement in a painting or drawing translates it into the perception of three-dimensional form.

Kress and Van Leeuwen (1996) were inspired by Halliday's (1985) conceptualization of language to view images as the final component of speech acts. Halliday identified four basic functions of pictures: they can demand products or services, offer good services, request information, or deliver information. For each image, there is always a potential counter-argument. Kress and Van Leeuwen argued that images fulfill both "offer" and "demand" functions, depending on how they engage the viewer.

Visuals can thus be interpreted as referring to actual dialogues. For instance, in the image *Words Fail to Speak*, we see a woman gazing directly at the viewer. This direct visual address engages the observer, even without any explicit verbal or narrative cues. Kress and Van Leeuwen suggested that all poses in an image serve as resources for guiding the viewer's evaluation of the participant. The way an individual is depicted—whether looking up or down at the observer—plays a crucial role in how they are positioned within the visual context.

A few essential questions may arise when analyzing the meaning of stance:

- To what extent does the person occupy space in the image?
- Are they performing for the viewer, or are they self-contained?
- Is there an emphasis on relaxation or intensity?
- Does the pose suggest openness or closeness?
- If more than one person is present, how do their postures relate to one another?
- To what degree are they depicted as intimate, or is there a sense of distance?

By using this analytical framework, we can understand how gaze influences viewers' implicit interpretations of the image. The woman's intense gaze affirms both the object of her attention and her identity as the subject, revealing a profound connection between the individual and the world. This shared space between the viewer and the subject reflects both our mutual existence and our individual perspectives (Sobchack, V., 1992, p. 85). From this perspective, the woman's deep suffering, though unspoken, is clearly communicated through her facial expression. Her gaze is focused inward, symbolizing the path her heart follows as it recedes from her soul. In essence, the silence of the image speaks volumes.

To fully comprehend the image's meaning, we should consider the fundamental features of the objects depicted. The woman, the trees, and the field of flowers all suggest stillness. Her expression indicates she is lost in thought, perhaps exploring her own imagination.

The imagery here strongly resonates with Rumi's poetry:

In the garden,
I see only your face;
From trees and blossoms
I inhale only your fragrance.
(Rumi: Bridge to the Soul, p.43)

This excerpt is drawn from Rumi's poem *Intoxicated by Love*, where he elegantly links a woman with the fragrance of flowers, expressing his admiration for her through metaphor. The line "I inhale only your fragrance" exemplifies *overlexicalization*, where the focus on one particular scent—the woman's—underscores its uniqueness, despite the presence of other fragrances, such as those from the flowers and trees around her.

Kevin Lynch observed that certain images convey a sense of depth, suggesting there is more than what the eye and ear can perceive at first glance (Kevin Lynch,1990, p. 6). In Rumi's work, this idea comes to life: inhaling the fragrance of a woman becomes a metaphor for perceiving beyond the physical world, engaging all the senses and expanding one's understanding of existence.

Enough words, Friend,
You can make the ear see.

Speak the rest of this poem
In that language.
(Rumi: Bridge to the Soul, p. 52, Lines 19-21)

"Words fail to speak" captures the essence of why some people have the most expressive eyes and smiles. Even though they work hard to mask their pain behind a smile, the depth of that pain remains visible in their eyes. In response to someone who once asked Rumi, "Isn't it strange that you talk about silence so much?", Rumi replied, "The radiant one inside me has never said a word."

Rumi frequently emphasizes silence, particularly at the ends of his poems, where words return to the silence from which they emerged. This focus on silence is one of his defining qualities, allowing him to convey profound truths. Through his poetry, Rumi illustrates how suffering can transform a person into one of God's most beautiful creations, even as it can also lead to deep destruction. The Qur'an reminds us, "We are all returning." In the pursuit of truth, humans encounter both joy and suffering before ultimately leaving the tavern—a metaphor for life's tumultuous yet glorious journey. Rumi suggests that while the tavern can be a perilous place, one should never conceal their heart.

Consider the difference
In our actions and God's actions.

We often ask, "Why did you do that?"
Or "Why did I act like that?"

We do act, and yet everything we do
Is God's creative action.

We look back and analyze the events
Of our lives, but there is another way
Of seeing, a backward-and-forward-at-once
Vision, that is not rationally understandable.

Only God can understand it.
Satan made the excuse, "You caused me to fall,"
Whereas Adam said to God, "We did this."
To ourselves. After this repentance,
God asked Adam, since all is within
My foreknowledge, why didn't you
Defend yourself with that reason?

(Rumi: Bridge to the Soul, Lines 1-17)

Some people give thanks to God for the suffering they have endured, recognising that without such trials, they would never have tasted the fruits of life. *Oubaitori* (桜梅桃甚), a traditional Japanese proverb, reflects this concept by highlighting the distinct growth patterns of four spring-blooming trees—plum, cherry, apricot, and peach. Each tree blooms at its own pace, producing different fruits and flowers. The deeper meaning of *Oubaitori* is that everyone matures at their own rate, and we should cherish our unique journey rather than compare ourselves to others.

Nature embodies this wisdom, as no two trees grow in exactly the same way. Even when they appear distant from each other, each tree appreciates its individuality and growth. The beauty of God's creation shines through in this natural diversity. Consider the example of *Baker's Globe Mallow* (Lliamna Baker), a plant with a hard shell that only germinates after a wildfire has shattered its outer layer. Despite its dormancy for up to a century, the plant's growth is triggered by the fire's destructive force, which reveals its hidden beauty. Similarly, in life, painful trials can break open our hardened shells, allowing us to discover strength and beauty we never knew we had.

This plant's process mirrors the way God sometimes uses trials to break open the shells of our hearts, offering us the opportunity to grow and emerge into the light. Sometimes, like the hatching of an egg, God must break our hearts repeatedly in order to guide us toward faith and renewal (Helwa, A., 2020, p. 287).

The Art of
READING
Images

Messenger of God

The process of analyzing the connection between form and content, particularly in relation to the recreated conditions of an artifact's creation and its viewing context, can be referred to as reading images. The reader of images compiles the potential meanings of style, subject matter, and media for both initial and subsequent audiences, while also considering the cultural and historical context in which the image was created. By situating the artwork within the contemporary struggles between temporal and religious powers, Schapiro illustrates how imagery can contribute to a new spiritual orientation, one that highlights the moral conflicts emerging directly from visual analysis. Schapiro's works, like all powerful readings, engage the mind and the eye, encouraging viewers to perceive things differently and approach familiar pieces with a spirit of exploration.

The Ornithomorphic Creator and Cosmic Imagery

The image of the ornithomorphic creator, often depicted as bird-like or sometimes humanoid, is an intriguing symbol. In some representations, the creator floats or hovers above a vast, dark, chaotic abyss, laying a single egg. This egg is destined to crack open, dividing into sections of white and yellow. The yellow yolk and the white of the egg are often interpreted symbolically as the sun and moon, or as the divided realms of heaven and earth. This imagery suggests that the spatiotemporal world itself originated from the cracked egg. In some depictions, multiple eggs are released, giving birth to celestial bodies such as the sun, moon, and stars, or the eggs are transformed into islands floating on the primordial sea.

The cosmic tree or mountain is often portrayed as the place where this celestial bird lays its eggs. Another interpretation links human, bird-like souls—particularly those of shamans, who are believed to be stars—to eggs that are placed in a nest atop the cosmic tree, which symbolises the world axis. These avian spirits were thought to possess the ability to sense variations in temperature, wind direction, barometric pressure, and other environmental factors, allowing them to know the optimal conditions for flying, roosting, and procreation. It was believed that solar birds carried life-giving water from the sky to the soil, and that the strongest birds, such as raptors, were responsible for lightning, thunder, and cyclones.

Symbolism of the Celestial Bird

In the Garuda Purana, Garuda, the king of birds, is portrayed in the form of a dialogue that offers insights into the afterlife. Similarly, Osiris, associated with the djed symbol, is frequently depicted with green or black skin, symbolizing both rebirth and the fertile mud of the Nile. He is also connected to the Bennu bird, a mythological figure that rises from the ashes, symbolizing resurrection. The Chinese Fèng huáng (凤凰), or Phoenix, embodies prosperity and good fortune. These diverse representations of the same bird across various cultures show a shared symbol—though named differently in each language and nation—that holds similar traits and characteristics.

The Book of Secret Wisdom speaks of Senzar, a language strongly connected to music, light, color, and number. This language is said to be the "language of the sun," based on symbolism. In mythology, it is often referred to as the "language of the birds" (Dushkova, 2015, p. 162). The Bennu bird of ancient Egypt, a powerful celestial being, was believed to possess the ability to regenerate itself both daily and once every 500 years. It was closely associated with the solar deity Atum. According to the myth, the name of the sun god was revealed through the image of the Bennu bird. As it rested on a rock, the Bennu bird cried out, revealing what had not yet been disclosed, much like the sun god himself, who was thought to have originated through self-generation.

Nature's Signals: Augury and Ornithological Knowledge

Before natural disasters such as volcanic eruptions, nature is believed to send distinct signals into the atmosphere. For example, tiny red stars might appear in the sky, indicating high atmospheric tension and the potential for earthquakes. Various animal and bird species are able to sense these changes, and, sensing their impending demise, they often flee the area. This premonition of disaster was also recognised in ancient Greek practices of augury, where ornithological knowledge played a significant role. The flight patterns and calls of birds were studied to predict future events. By observing the birds' movements and sounds, the ancient Greeks practiced this art of divination.

Birdsong, in particular, held great significance. The moment when certain birds began to sing or cry, signaling the approach of dawn, was seen as an essential indicator of the sun's rising. In this way, birds were believed to offer vital clues to the natural rhythms of the world, and their behavior was closely monitored as a means of understanding cosmic and earthly events.

Creative Writing Suggestions and Recommendations

The most effective means of communicating ideas is creativity and the arts. This book recognises the value of an open public space where the energy and potential of all the learners or observers involved can be explored and expressed. It does this by emphasising the significance of creative reading and writing for images. Everybody is creative, yet everyone uses creativity in various ways (Robinson, 2001, p. 12).

Reflecting on Different Perspectives:

1. You should start your analysis by discussing the various ways that individuals may interpret the same visuals. Many interpretations might disclose a great deal about personal prejudices, cultural origins, and individual experiences. Why these kinds of distinctions are unavoidable in some societies. How the world at large would be made aware of the

visuals that before may have disgusted or misled them, thanks to your study.

2. Examine how the interaction of word and image produces a deeper, more complex comprehension of the material. Which visuals are most effective for advertising but not for teaching?

Directing Audiences to Engage with Content:

Encourage Active Observation:

1. Before reading the text, advise viewers to take some time to pause looking at the photos. To help children develop a personal connection to the images, encourage them to jot down their initial feelings and ideas.

Facilitate Discussion:

1. Provide forums for thought or discussion around the pictures. Forums or group discussions can shed light on differing perspectives and enhance comprehension.

Integrate Multimodal Analysis:

Inspire viewers to examine various media formats, such as infographics and videos, in addition to photographs. They may be better able to evaluate and comprehend many kinds of content thanks to this multimodal approach. perspectives, and to be willing to change their minds after learning new knowledge.

Highlight the Impact of Context:

Examine how perception can be influenced by context. It might affect one's interpretation of an image to know its context and intended meaning. Tell us how you think the visuals you interpret can contribute to social harmony.

How can we teach people to change interpretations responsibly if they are provided by authority figures without appropriate validation?

Promote Open-Mindedness:

1. Encourage an atmosphere that values different interpretations. Urge viewers to think about many viewpoints and to be willing to change their minds about what they initially thought in light of new knowledge.

The Art of Reading Images seeks to improve audiences' capacity to critically connect with and analyze a wide range of content by leading them through this process and developing a greater appreciation for the interaction between visual and textual aspects.

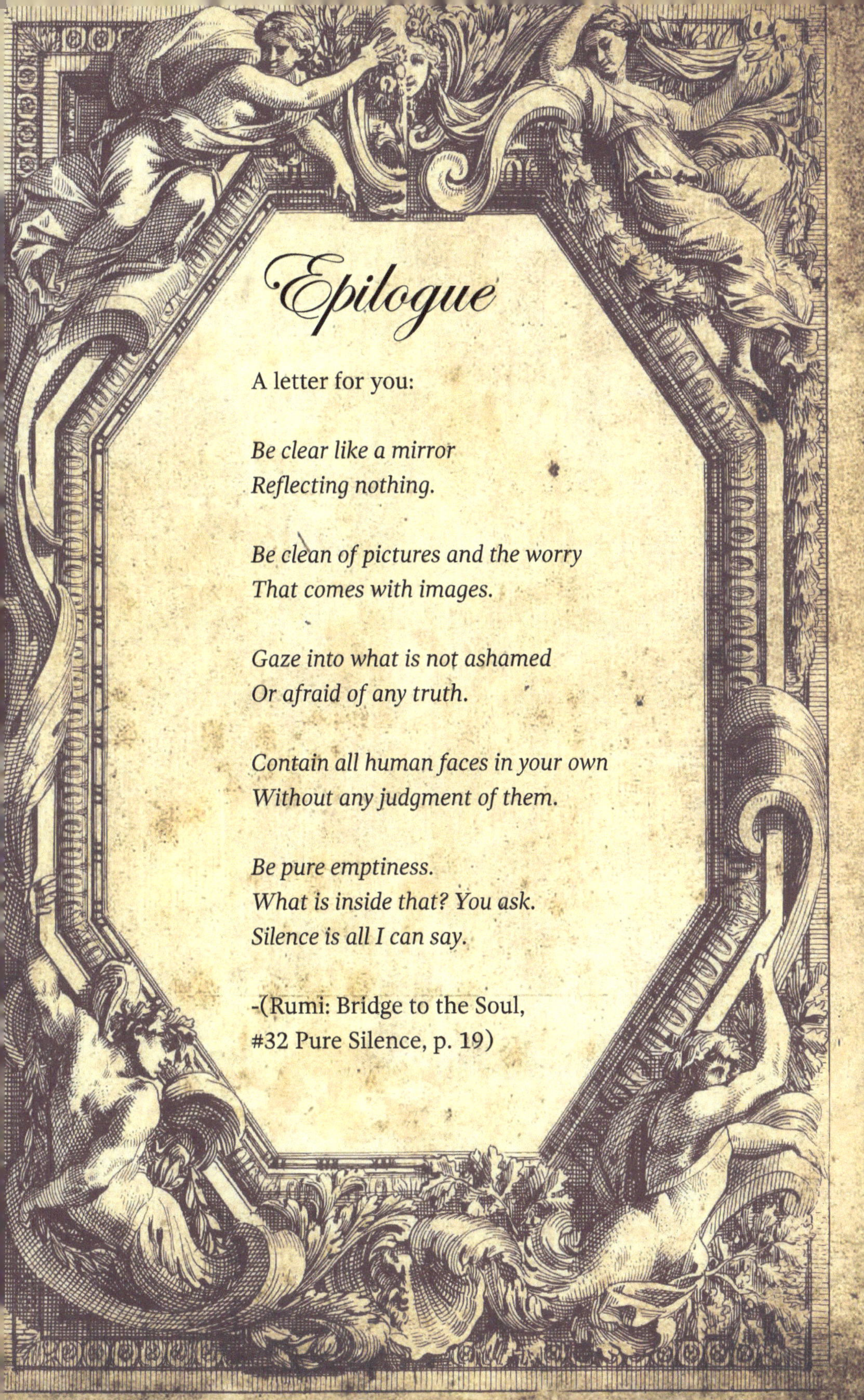

Epilogue

A letter for you:

Be clear like a mirror
Reflecting nothing.

Be clean of pictures and the worry
That comes with images.

Gaze into what is not ashamed
Or afraid of any truth.

Contain all human faces in your own
Without any judgment of them.

Be pure emptiness.
What is inside that? You ask.
Silence is all I can say.

-(Rumi: Bridge to the Soul,
#32 Pure Silence, p. 19)

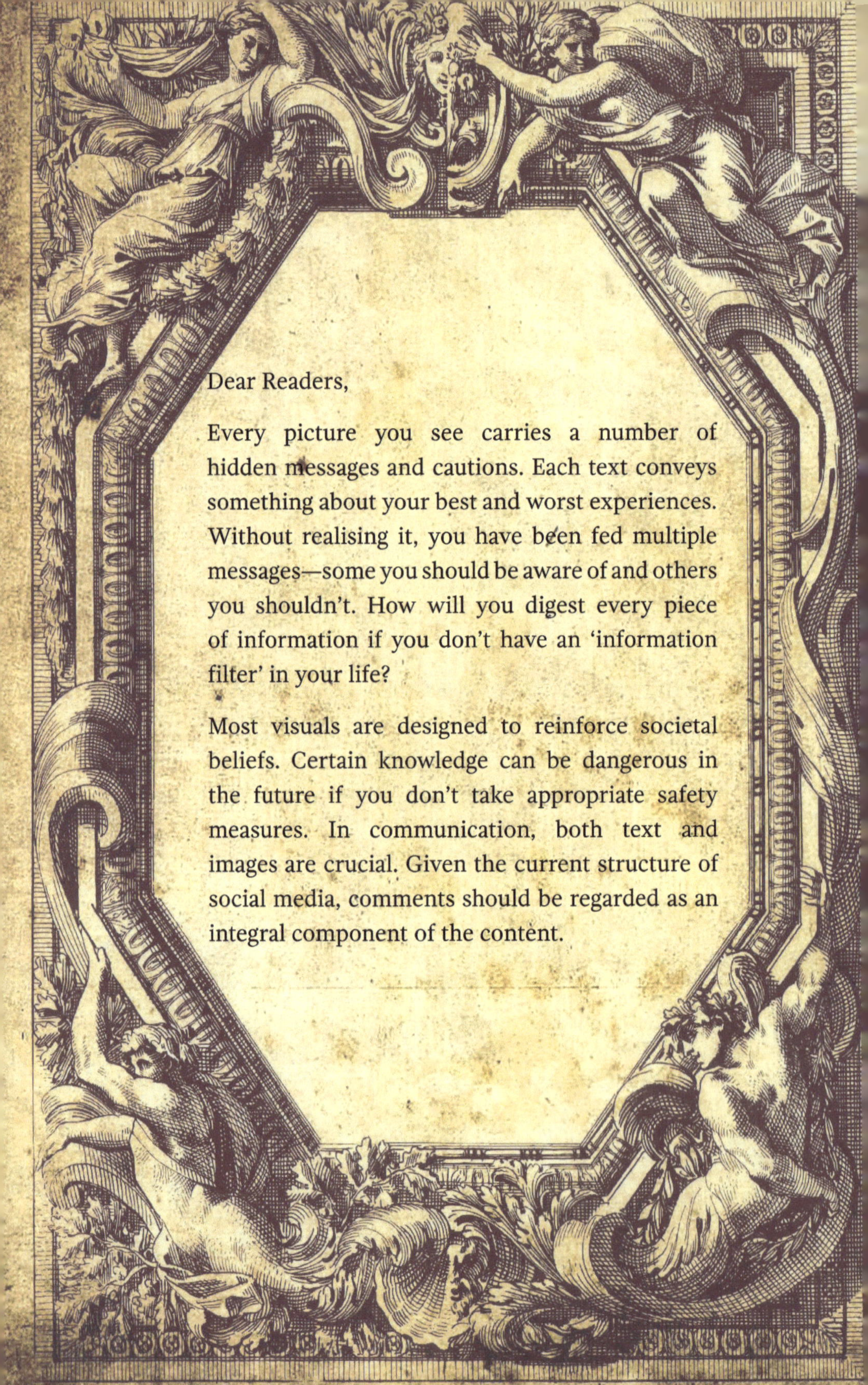

Dear Readers,

Every picture you see carries a number of hidden messages and cautions. Each text conveys something about your best and worst experiences. Without realising it, you have been fed multiple messages—some you should be aware of and others you shouldn't. How will you digest every piece of information if you don't have an 'information filter' in your life?

Most visuals are designed to reinforce societal beliefs. Certain knowledge can be dangerous in the future if you don't take appropriate safety measures. In communication, both text and images are crucial. Given the current structure of social media, comments should be regarded as an integral component of the content.

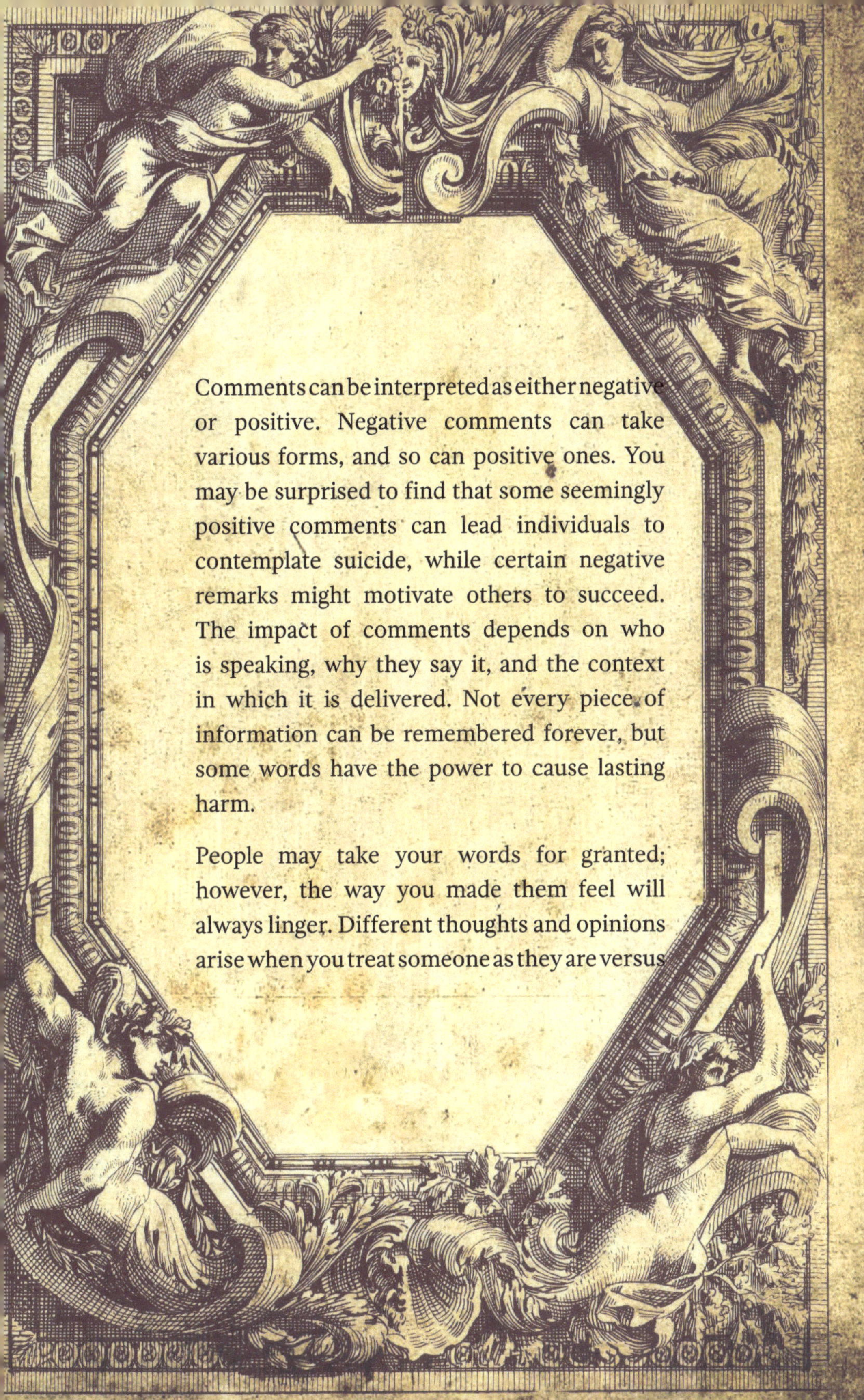

Comments can be interpreted as either negative or positive. Negative comments can take various forms, and so can positive ones. You may be surprised to find that some seemingly positive comments can lead individuals to contemplate suicide, while certain negative remarks might motivate others to succeed. The impact of comments depends on who is speaking, why they say it, and the context in which it is delivered. Not every piece of information can be remembered forever, but some words have the power to cause lasting harm.

People may take your words for granted; however, the way you made them feel will always linger. Different thoughts and opinions arise when you treat someone as they are versus

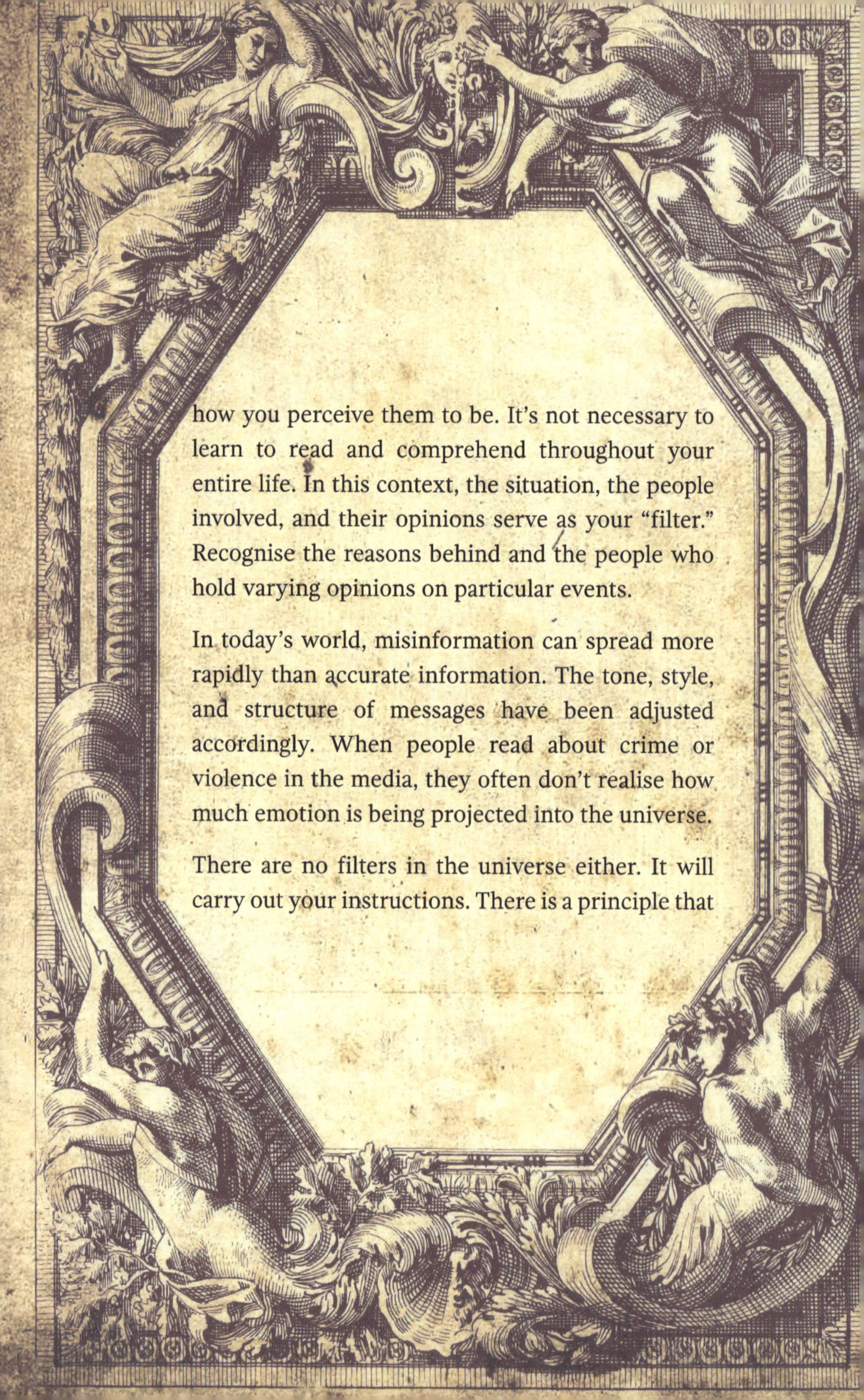

how you perceive them to be. It's not necessary to learn to read and comprehend throughout your entire life. In this context, the situation, the people involved, and their opinions serve as your "filter." Recognise the reasons behind and the people who hold varying opinions on particular events.

In today's world, misinformation can spread more rapidly than accurate information. The tone, style, and structure of messages have been adjusted accordingly. When people read about crime or violence in the media, they often don't realise how much emotion is being projected into the universe.

There are no filters in the universe either. It will carry out your instructions. There is a principle that

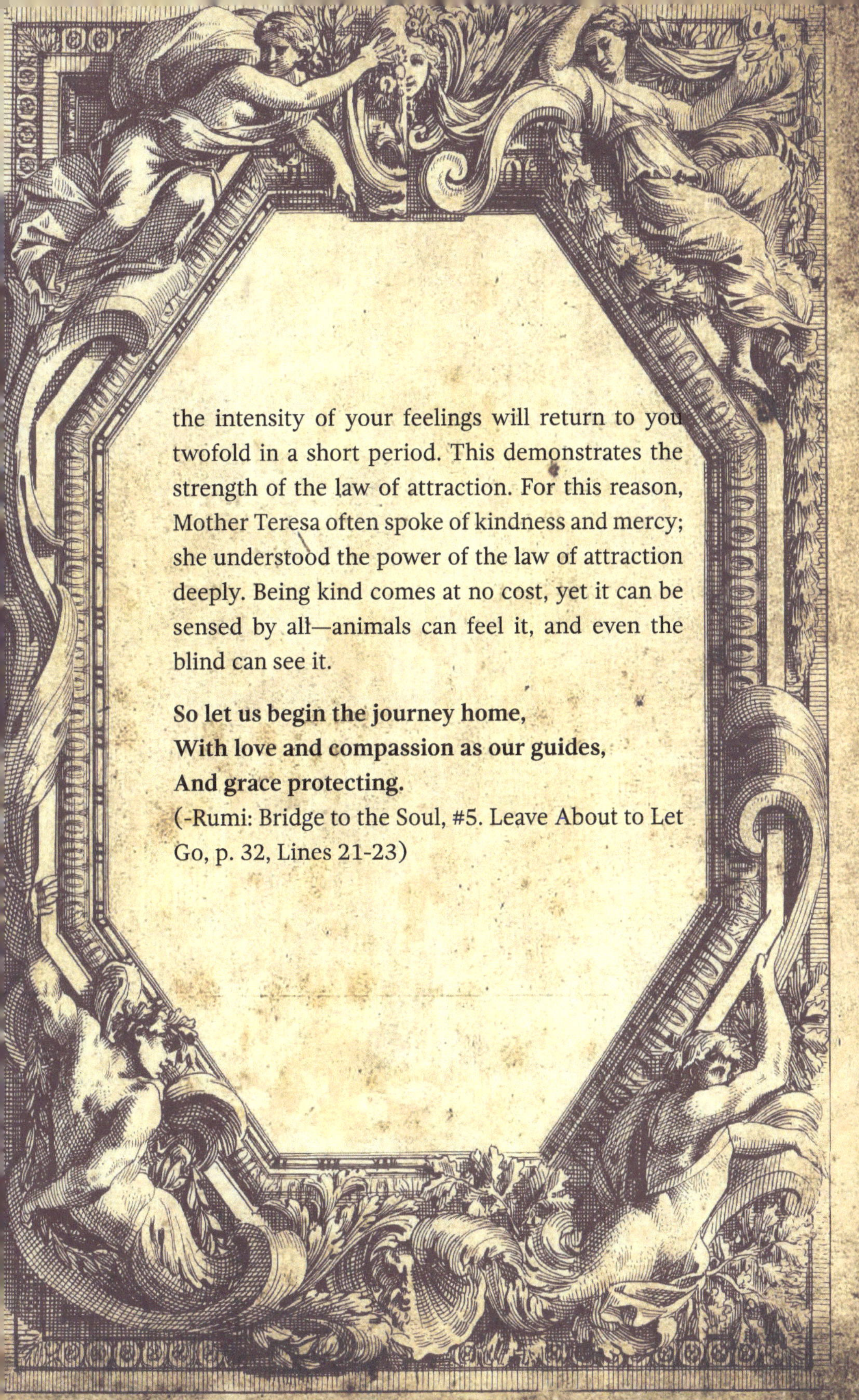

the intensity of your feelings will return to you twofold in a short period. This demonstrates the strength of the law of attraction. For this reason, Mother Teresa often spoke of kindness and mercy; she understood the power of the law of attraction deeply. Being kind comes at no cost, yet it can be sensed by all—animals can feel it, and even the blind can see it.

So let us begin the journey home,
With love and compassion as our guides,
And grace protecting.
(-Rumi: Bridge to the Soul, #5. Leave About to Let Go, p. 32, Lines 21-23)

References

Barks, C. (2007). *Rumi: Bridge to the Soul: Journeys into the Music and Silence of the Heart*. Translations by Coleman Barks with A.J. Arberry and Nevit Ergin. HarperCollins e-book.

Boeri, M. D., Kanayama, Y. Y., & Mittelmann, J. (2018). *Soul and Mind in Greek Thought: Psychological Issues in Plato and Aristotle*. Springer.

Byrne, R. (2018). *The Secret: Dare to Dream*. Beyond Words, Hillsboro, Oregon.

Charles, F. (2019, November 22). Kress and Van Leeuwen's *Reading Images: The Grammar of Visual Design* (1996). Vrije Universiteit Amsterdam/Rijksuniversiteit Leiden (OSL), The Netherlands. https://5metrosdepoemas.com/index.php/noticias/22-mapamundi/684-kress-and-van-leeuwen-s-reading-images-the-grammar-of-visual-design-1996

Chopra, D. (1993). *The Love Poems of Rumi*. Edited by Deepak Chopra and Fereydoun Kia. Harmony Books, New York.

Danny, M. Vaughn. *Principles of Images Interpretation*. Retrieved from http://seros.us/moodle/

Ezquerra, J. E. (2016). Kress, Gunther R. (2010). *Multimodality: A Social Semiotic Approach to Contemporary Communication*. *Revista Latinoamericana de Estudios del Discurso*, 12(1), 124. https://doi.org/10.35956/v.12.n1.2012.p.124-130.

Forceville, C. (1999). Educating the Eye?: Kress and Van Leeuwen's *Reading Images: The Grammar of Visual Design* (1996). *Language and Literature*, 8(2), 163-178.

Galef, D., & Hashimoto, J. (2012). *Japanese Proverbs: Wit and Wisdom*. Tuttle Publishing.

Gardes Collees, M. (2008). *Michel Pastourean Black: The History of a Color*. Translated from the French by Jody Gladding. Library of Congress Cataloging-in-Publication Data. Princeton University Press, Princeton and Oxford.

Grainger, T., Goouch, K., & Lambirth, A. (2005). *Creativity and Writing: Developing Voice and Verse in the Classroom*. Routledge, Taylor & Francis Group.

Helwa, A. (2020). *Secrets of Divine Love: A Spiritual Journey into the Heart of Islam*. Naulit Publishing, United States.

Hermawan, B. (2011). Review: *Reading Images: The Grammar of Visual Design*. *CONAPLIN Journal: Indonesian Journal of Applied Linguistics*, 1(1), 147-148.

Kress, G., & Van Leeuwen, T. (1990/1996). *Reading Images: The Grammar of Visual Design*. Routledge.

Kress, G., & Van Leeuwen, T. (2001). *Multimodal Discourse: The Modes and Media of Contemporary Communication*. Edward Arnold.

Kress, G. (2010). *Multimodality: A Social Semiotic Approach to Contemporary Communication*. Routledge.

Lynch, K. (1990). *The Image of the City*. Massachusetts Institute of Technology Press.

Machin, D., & Mayr, A. (2012). *How to Do Critical Discourse Analysis: A Multimodal Introduction*. Sage Publications Ltd.

Mangali, G., & David, A. (2018). Enjoying and Enduring: A Gaman (我慢) Experience of Filipino Doctoral Science Students in Japan as "Teachers as Learners." *National Journal of Research Studies in Education*, 7(4), 63-79.

Marion, J. S., & Crowder, J. W. (2013). *Visual Research: A Concise Introduction to Thinking Visually*. https://ci.nii.ac.jp/ncid/BB12054198

Midalia, S. (1999). Textualizing Gender. In *Interpretations*, 32(1), 27-32.

Rappengluck, M. A. (2009). Heavenly Messengers: The Role of Birds in the Cosmographies and the Cosmovisions of Ancient Cultures. In *Cosmology Across Cultures* (Vol. 409, pp. 1-10). J. A. Rubino Martín, J. A. Belmonte, F. Prada, & A. Alberdi (Eds.). Online at: https://www.academia.edu/2545086/Heavenly_Messengers_The_Role_of_Birds_in_the_Cosmographies_and_the_Cosmovisions_of_Ancient_Cultures

Robinson, K. (2001). *Out of Our Minds: Learning to Be Creative*. Capstone Publishing.

Rosewell, R. (1860). *Stained Glass*. St. Mary, Hanley Castle, Worcestershire.

Sears, E., & Thomas, K. Thelma. (2002). *Reading Medieval Images: The Art Historian and the Object*. The University of Michigan Press.

Sobchack, V. (1992). *The Address of the Eye: A Phenomenology of Film Experience*. Princeton University Press.

Wood, E., & Subrahmanyam, S. V. (2006). *The Garuda Purana Sarodhhara*. United States. https://www.pdfdrive.com/the-garuda-purana-e894131.html

Ziegler, G. (1986). *Tarot: Mirror of the Soul*. Samuel Weiser, Inc., York Beach, Maine.

Zinovia, D. (2015). *The Book of Secret Wisdom: The Prophetic Record of Human Destiny and Evolution*. Translated from Russian. Stansty Liubvi: Zvezda Vostoka, Novosibirsk.

eChineseLearning Live Teachers from China. (2023, January 26). *Chinese Culture: What Are the Differences Between the Fèng Huáng and the Pheonix?* eChineseLearning Live Teachers from China. https://www.echineselearning.com/blog/chinese-culture-what-are-the-differences-between-the-feng-huang-and-the-pheonix#:~:text=F%C3%A8ng%20Hu%C3%A1ng%2C%20or%20Chinese%20phoenix&text=In%20fact%2C%20the%20phoenix%20is,bring%20peace%20to%20the%20world.